This Book Is Belongs To

Lucia Johnson!! ☺☺

Panista Publishing

Hello God!
It's Me Again

Today I Learned ...

that dont use weapons in a battle use ♡LOVE♡

Today I'm Grateful For ...

My family and friends and that I have incredible people looking out for me that love me so much!

My Prayers Today ...

Dear God
thank you for giving me such amazing people that care for me and your love for me!

Amen!

Hello God!
It's Me Again

Today I Learned ...

That the fact I can go on holiday is !MEGA!

Today I'm Grateful For ...

My family and for the Everyardys for giving us a cottage to stay in!

My Prayers Today ...

Dear God, I love you for everything!

Amen!

Hello God!
It's Me Again

Today I Learned ...

Today I'm Grateful For ...

My Prayers Today ...

Amen!

Hello God!
It's Me Again

Today I Learned ...

Today I'm Grateful For ...

My Prayers Today ...

Amen!

Hello God!
It's Me Again

Today I Learned ...

Today I'm Grateful For ...

My Prayers Today ...

Amen!

Hello God!
It's Me Again

Today I Learned ...

Today I'm Grateful For ...

My Prayers Today ...

Amen!

Hello God!
It's Me Again

Today I Learned ...

Today I'm Grateful For ...

My Prayers Today ...

Amen!

Hello God!
It's Me Again

Today I Learned ...

Today I'm Grateful For ...

My Prayers Today ...

Amen!

Hello God!
It's Me Again

Today I Learned ...

Today I'm Grateful For ...

My Prayers Today ...

Amen!

Hello God!
It's Me Again

Today I Learned ...

Today I'm Grateful For ...

My Prayers Today ...

Amen!

Hello God!
It's Me Again

Today I Learned ...

Today I'm Grateful For ...

My Prayers Today ...

Amen!

Hello God!
It's Me Again

Today I Learned ...

Today I'm Grateful For ...

My Prayers Today ...

Amen!

Hello God!
It's Me Again

Today I Learned ...

Today I'm Grateful For ...

My Prayers Today ...

Amen!

Hello God!
It's Me Again

Today I Learned ...

Today I'm Grateful For ...

My Prayers Today ...

Amen!

Hello God!
It's Me Again

Today I Learned ...

Today I'm Grateful For ...

My Prayers Today ...

Amen!

Hello God!
It's Me Again

Today I Learned ...

Today I'm Grateful For ...

My Prayers Today ...

Amen!

Hello God!
It's Me Again

Today I Learned ...

Today I'm Grateful For ...

My Prayers Today ...

Amen!

Hello God!
It's Me Again

Today I Learned ...

Today I'm Grateful For ...

My Prayers Today ...

Amen!

Hello God!
It's Me Again

Today I Learned ...

Today I'm Grateful For ...

My Prayers Today ...

Amen!

Hello God!
It's Me Again

Today I Learned ...

Today I'm Grateful For ...

My Prayers Today ...

Amen!

Hello God!
It's Me Again

Today I Learned ...

Today I'm Grateful For ...

My Prayers Today ...

Amen!

Hello God!
It's Me Again

Today I Learned ...

Today I'm Grateful For ...

My Prayers Today ...

Amen!

Hello God!
It's Me Again

Today I Learned ...

Today I'm Grateful For ...

My Prayers Today ...

Amen!

Hello God!
It's Me Again

Today I Learned ...

Today I'm Grateful For ...

My Prayers Today ...

Amen!

Hello God!
It's Me Again

Today I Learned ...

Today I'm Grateful For ...

My Prayers Today ...

Amen!

Hello God!
It's Me Again

Today I Learned ...

Today I'm Grateful For ...

My Prayers Today ...

Amen!

Hello God!
It's Me Again

Today I Learned ...

Today I'm Grateful For ...

My Prayers Today ...

Amen!

Hello God!
It's Me Again

Today I Learned ...

Today I'm Grateful For ...

My Prayers Today ...

Amen!

Hello God!
It's Me Again

Today I Learned ...

Today I'm Grateful For ...

My Prayers Today ...

Amen!

Hello God!
It's Me Again

Today I Learned ...

Today I'm Grateful For ...

My Prayers Today ...

Amen!

Hello God!
It's Me Again

Today I Learned ...

Today I'm Grateful For ...

My Prayers Today ...

Amen!

Hello God!
It's Me Again

Today I Learned ...

Today I'm Grateful For ...

My Prayers Today ...

Amen!

Hello God!
It's Me Again

Today I Learned ...

Today I'm Grateful For ...

My Prayers Today ...

Amen!

Hello God!
It's Me Again

Today I Learned ...

Today I'm Grateful For ...

My Prayers Today ...

Amen!

Hello God!
It's Me Again

Today I Learned ...

Today I'm Grateful For ...

My Prayers Today ...

Amen!

Hello God!
It's Me Again

Today I Learned ...

Today I'm Grateful For ...

My Prayers Today ...

Amen!

Hello God!
It's Me Again

Today I Learned ...

Today I'm Grateful For ...

My Prayers Today ...

Amen!

Hello God!
It's Me Again

Today I Learned ...

Today I'm Grateful For ...

My Prayers Today ...

Amen!

Hello God!
It's Me Again

Today I Learned ...

Today I'm Grateful For ...

My Prayers Today ...

Amen!

Hello God!
It's Me Again

Today I Learned ...

Today I'm Grateful For ...

My Prayers Today ...

Amen!

Hello God!
It's Me Again

Today I Learned ...

Today I'm Grateful For ...

My Prayers Today ...

Amen!

Hello God!
It's Me Again

Today I Learned ...

Today I'm Grateful For ...

My Prayers Today ...

Amen!

Hello God!
It's Me Again

Today I Learned ...

Today I'm Grateful For ...

My Prayers Today ...

Amen!

Hello God!
It's Me Again

Today I Learned ...

Today I'm Grateful For ...

My Prayers Today ...

Amen!

Hello God!
It's Me Again

Today I Learned ...

Today I'm Grateful For ...

My Prayers Today ...

Amen!

Hello God!
It's Me Again

Today I Learned ...

Today I'm Grateful For ...

My Prayers Today ...

Amen!

Hello God!
It's Me Again

Today I Learned ...

Today I'm Grateful For ...

My Prayers Today ...

Amen!

Hello God!
It's Me Again

Today I Learned ...

Today I'm Grateful For ...

My Prayers Today ...

Amen!

Hello God!
It's Me Again

Today I Learned ...

Today I'm Grateful For ...

My Prayers Today ...

Amen!

Hello God!
It's Me Again

Today I Learned ...

Today I'm Grateful For ...

My Prayers Today ...

Amen!

Hello God!
It's Me Again

Today I Learned ...

Today I'm Grateful For ...

My Prayers Today ...

Amen!

Hello God!
It's Me Again

Today I Learned ...

Today I'm Grateful For ...

My Prayers Today ...

Amen!

Hello God!
It's Me Again

Today I Learned ...

Today I'm Grateful For ...

My Prayers Today ...

Amen!

Hello God!
It's Me Again

Today I Learned ...

Today I'm Grateful For ...

My Prayers Today ...

Amen!

Hello God!
It's Me Again

Today I Learned ...

Today I'm Grateful For ...

My Prayers Today ...

Amen!

Hello God!
It's Me Again

Today I Learned ...

Today I'm Grateful For ...

My Prayers Today ...

Amen!

Hello God!
It's Me Again

Today I Learned ...

Today I'm Grateful For ...

My Prayers Today ...

Amen!

Hello God!
It's Me Again

Today I Learned ...

Today I'm Grateful For ...

My Prayers Today ...

Amen!

Hello God!
It's Me Again

Today I Learned ...

Today I'm Grateful For ...

My Prayers Today ...

Amen!

Hello God!
It's Me Again

Today I Learned ...

Today I'm Grateful For ...

My Prayers Today ...

Amen!

Hello God!
It's Me Again

Today I Learned ...

Today I'm Grateful For ...

My Prayers Today ...

Amen!

Hello God!
It's Me Again

Today I Learned ...

Today I'm Grateful For ...

My Prayers Today ...

Amen!

Hello God!
It's Me Again

Today I Learned ...

Today I'm Grateful For ...

My Prayers Today ...

Amen!

Hello God!
It's Me Again

Today I Learned ...

Today I'm Grateful For ...

My Prayers Today ...

Amen!

Hello God!
It's Me Again

Today I Learned ...

Today I'm Grateful For ...

My Prayers Today ...

Amen!

Hello God!
It's Me Again

Today I Learned ...

Today I'm Grateful For ...

My Prayers Today ...

Amen!

Hello God!
It's Me Again

Today I Learned …

Today I'm Grateful For …

My Prayers Today …

Amen!

Hello God!
It's Me Again

Today I Learned ...

Today I'm Grateful For ...

My Prayers Today ...

Amen!

Hello God!
It's Me Again

Today I Learned ...

Today I'm Grateful For ...

My Prayers Today ...

Amen!

Hello God!
It's Me Again

Today I Learned ...

Today I'm Grateful For ...

My Prayers Today ...

Amen!

Hello God!
It's Me Again

Today I Learned ...

Today I'm Grateful For ...

My Prayers Today ...

Amen!

Hello God!
It's Me Again

Today I Learned ...

Today I'm Grateful For ...

My Prayers Today ...

Amen!

Hello God!
It's Me Again

Today I Learned ...

Today I'm Grateful For ...

My Prayers Today ...

Amen!

Hello God!
It's Me Again

Today I Learned ...

Today I'm Grateful For ...

My Prayers Today ...

Amen!

Hello God!
It's Me Again

Today I Learned ...

Today I'm Grateful For ...

My Prayers Today ...

Amen!

Hello God!
It's Me Again

Today I Learned ...

Today I'm Grateful For ...

My Prayers Today ...

Amen!

Hello God!
It's Me Again

Today I Learned ...

Today I'm Grateful For ...

My Prayers Today ...

Amen!

Hello God!
It's Me Again

Today I Learned ...

Today I'm Grateful For ...

My Prayers Today ...

Amen!

Hello God!
It's Me Again

Today I Learned ...

Today I'm Grateful For ...

My Prayers Today ...

Amen!

Hello God!
It's Me Again

Today I Learned ...

Today I'm Grateful For ...

My Prayers Today ...

Amen!

Hello God!
It's Me Again

Today I Learned ...

Today I'm Grateful For ...

My Prayers Today ...

Amen!

Hello God!
It's Me Again

Today I Learned ...

Today I'm Grateful For ...

My Prayers Today ...

Amen!

Hello God!
It's Me Again

Today I Learned ...

Today I'm Grateful For ...

My Prayers Today ...

Amen!

Hello God!
It's Me Again

Today I Learned ...

Today I'm Grateful For ...

My Prayers Today ...

Amen!

Hello God!
It's Me Again

Today I Learned ...

Today I'm Grateful For ...

My Prayers Today ...

Amen!

Hello God!
It's Me Again

Today I Learned ...

Today I'm Grateful For ...

My Prayers Today ...

Amen!

Hello God!
It's Me Again

Today I Learned ...

Today I'm Grateful For ...

My Prayers Today ...

Amen!

Hello God!
It's Me Again

Today I Learned ...

Today I'm Grateful For ...

My Prayers Today ...

Amen!

Hello God!
It's Me Again

Today I Learned ...

Today I'm Grateful For ...

My Prayers Today ...

Amen!

Hello God!
It's Me Again

Today I Learned ...

Today I'm Grateful For ...

My Prayers Today ...

Amen!

Hello God!
It's Me Again

Today I Learned ...

Today I'm Grateful For ...

My Prayers Today ...

Amen!

Hello God!
It's Me Again

Today I Learned ...

Today I'm Grateful For ...

My Prayers Today ...

Amen!

Hello God!
It's Me Again

Today I Learned ...

Today I'm Grateful For ...

My Prayers Today ...

Amen!

Hello God!
It's Me Again

Today I Learned ...

Today I'm Grateful For ...

My Prayers Today ...

Amen!

Hello God!
It's Me Again

Today I Learned ...

Today I'm Grateful For ...

My Prayers Today ...

Amen!

Hello God!
It's Me Again

Today I Learned ...

Today I'm Grateful For ...

My Prayers Today ...

Amen!

Hello God!
It's Me Again

Today I Learned ...

Today I'm Grateful For ...

My Prayers Today ...

Amen!

Hello God!
It's Me Again

Today I Learned ...

Today I'm Grateful For ...

My Prayers Today ...

Amen!

Hello God!
It's Me Again

Today I Learned ...

Today I'm Grateful For ...

My Prayers Today ...

Amen!

Hello God!
It's Me Again

Today I Learned ...

Today I'm Grateful For ...

My Prayers Today ...

Amen!

Hello God!
It's Me Again

Today I Learned ...

Today I'm Grateful For ...

My Prayers Today ...

Amen!

Hello God!
It's Me Again

Today I Learned ...

Today I'm Grateful For ...

My Prayers Today ...

Amen!

Hello God!
It's Me Again

Today I Learned ...

Today I'm Grateful For ...

My Prayers Today ...

Amen!

Hello God!
It's Me Again

Today I Learned ...

Today I'm Grateful For ...

My Prayers Today ...

Amen!

Hello God!
It's Me Again

Today I Learned ...

Today I'm Grateful For ...

My Prayers Today ...

Amen!

Hello God!
It's Me Again

Today I Learned ...

Today I'm Grateful For ...

My Prayers Today ...

Amen!

Hello God!
It's Me Again

Today I Learned ...

Today I'm Grateful For ...

My Prayers Today ...

Amen!

Hello God!
It's Me Again

Today I Learned ...

Today I'm Grateful For ...

My Prayers Today ...

Amen!

Hello God!
It's Me Again

Today I Learned ...

Today I'm Grateful For ...

My Prayers Today ...

Amen!

Printed in Great Britain
by Amazon